A *Doonesbury* book by

G. B. Trudeau

A Farewell To Alms

Selected Cartoons from
THE WRECK OF THE "RUSTY NAIL"
Volume 1

FAWCETT CREST • NEW YORK

A Fawcett Crest Book
Published by Ballantine Books
Copyright © 1981, 1982, 1983 by G.B. Trudeau

Library of Congress Catalog Card Number: 82-83139

ISBN 0-449-20197-X

This book comprises a portion of THE WRECK OF THE ''RUSTY NAIL''
and is reprinted by arrangement with Holt, Rinehart and Winston

Manufactured in the United States of America

First Ballantine Books Edition: May 1984

10 9 8 7 6 5 4 3 2 1

A Farewell
To Alms

YOU HAVEN'T SAID A WORD ABOUT MY NEW BIKINI, SIR.

DON'T RUSH ME.

TODAY "TIME" MAGAZINE PUBLISHED ITS SIXTH LENGTHY EXCERPT FROM THE CONTINUING MEMOIRS OF HENRY KISSINGER. THIS YEAR'S INSTALLMENTS ARE FROM THE LATEST KISSINGER VOLUME, "YEARS OF WHITEWASH" ALSO PUBLISHED BY "TIME."

MEET HENRY GRUNWALD, EDITOR OF "TIME." MR. GRUNWALD, ISN'T YOUR MAGAZINE'S FASCINATION WITH KISSINGER BEGINNING TO TURN INTO AN OBSESSION?

NO, I THINK IT'S SOMETHING RATHER MORE SPECIAL.

MY EDITORS AND I HAVE BECOME THE KEEPERS OF THE KISSINGER FLAME. WE DOTE ON HIM, WE CONSULT HIM, WE WORSHIPFULLY TRACK HIS EVERY MOVE. HIS VIEW OF HISTORY, TO WHICH WE HOLD ALL THE RIGHTS, IS GOSPEL— UNEXAMINED AND IMMACULATE.

I SEE. SO IT'S MORE LIKE AN ORGANIZED RELIGION.

RIGHT. IN FACT, WE'RE APPLYING FOR TAX-EXEMPT STATUS.

DR. DAN, IN YOUR PREFACE TO "THE MELLOW PARENT", YOU MAKE THE POINT THAT THE BIGGEST DECISION A COUPLE WILL EVER FACE IS **WHEN** TO BECOME PARENTS, RIGHT?

THAT'S RIGHT, MARK. TIMING IS THE HOT SUBJECT TODAY, ESPECIALLY TO WOMEN OVER 30. MANY OF THEM ARE TRYING TO BUILD CAREERS, BUT THEY HEAR THEIR BIOLOGICAL CLOCKS TICKING AWAY.